THE WORLD'S CITIES

TOKYO

CREDITS

Series Editor: Nicolas Wright
Series Designer: Kris Flynn
Picture Researcher: Kathy Brandt

Text by Mitsuaki Usami and Cheung Hon-Chung
of Chinatech Limited, London

Published by Chartwell Books Inc., A
Division of Book Sales Inc., 110 Enterprise
Avenue, Secaucus, New Jersey 07094

© Marshall Cavendish Limited 1978

Produced by Theorem Publishing Limited,
71/73 Great Portland Street, London W1N 5DH
for Marshall Cavendish Books Limited

Printed in Great Britain

First printing 1978

ISBN 0 89009 158 7

THE WORLD'S CITIES

TOKYO

CHARTWELL
BOOKS INC.

CONTENTS

Introduction to Tokyo

Tokyo, the capital of Japan, is an endless display of fireworks; the sparks fly in every direction but never last long enough to be recalled in detail – an oriental firecracker ignited by the ultra-modern electronic lighter.

The city is a unique blend of leisurely eastern philosophy with western materialism. It is a place of contrast, a place of surprise. Where else would one find traditionally kimono-clad passengers relaxing in 125 mile-an-hour trains? Where else would a classical 1,000 year old theatre compete for audiences with a punk rock disco?

Custom may die hard in latter-day Tokyo but bricks and mortar seem to change as rapidly as the days themselves. The repeated devastation of fire, earthquake and the Second World War air raids have made Tokyo probably the world's most up-to-date city. Scarcely an old building remains: every office block, every store, every apartment, proclaims Tokyo's brash modernity. The steel, glass and concrete of the new age are indeed generations away from the rapidly dwindling relics of ancient Tokyo.

Tokyo is now estimated to be the most populous city in the world; any rush hour commuter will fervently agree, although wishing it were otherwise. It is also fast-moving, exhilarating and mysterious.

This book captures the excitement and the wonder of the Tokyo of the 1970s. Informed, succinct text married to a breathtaking series of photographs make it essential reading for anyone wishing to learn more of this enigmatic city.

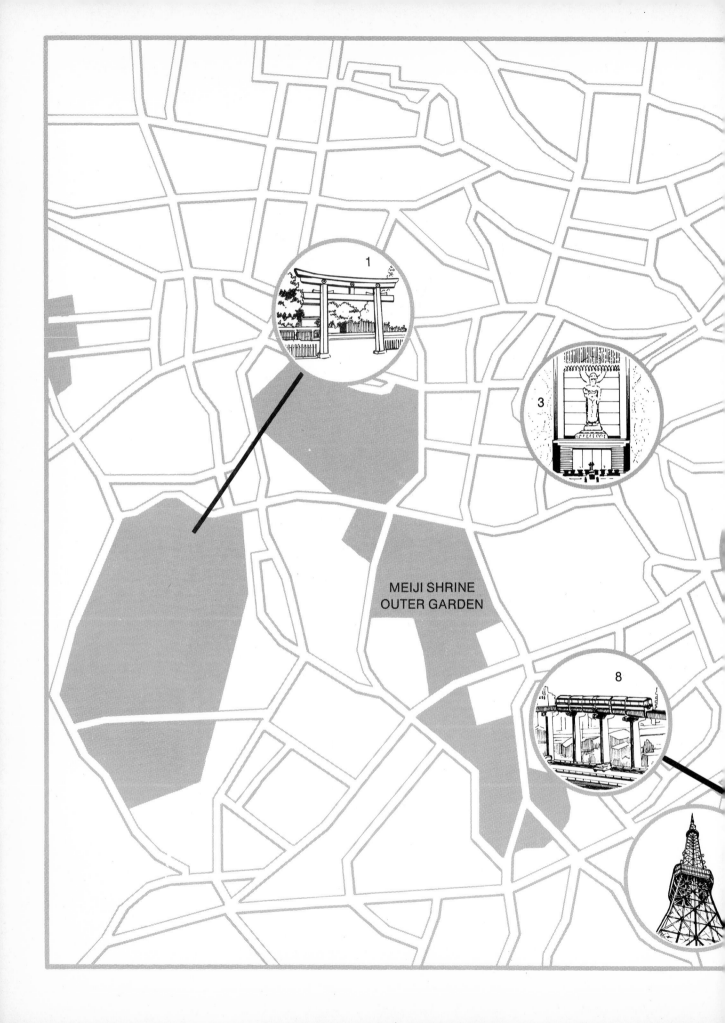

MEIJI SHRINE
OUTER GARDEN

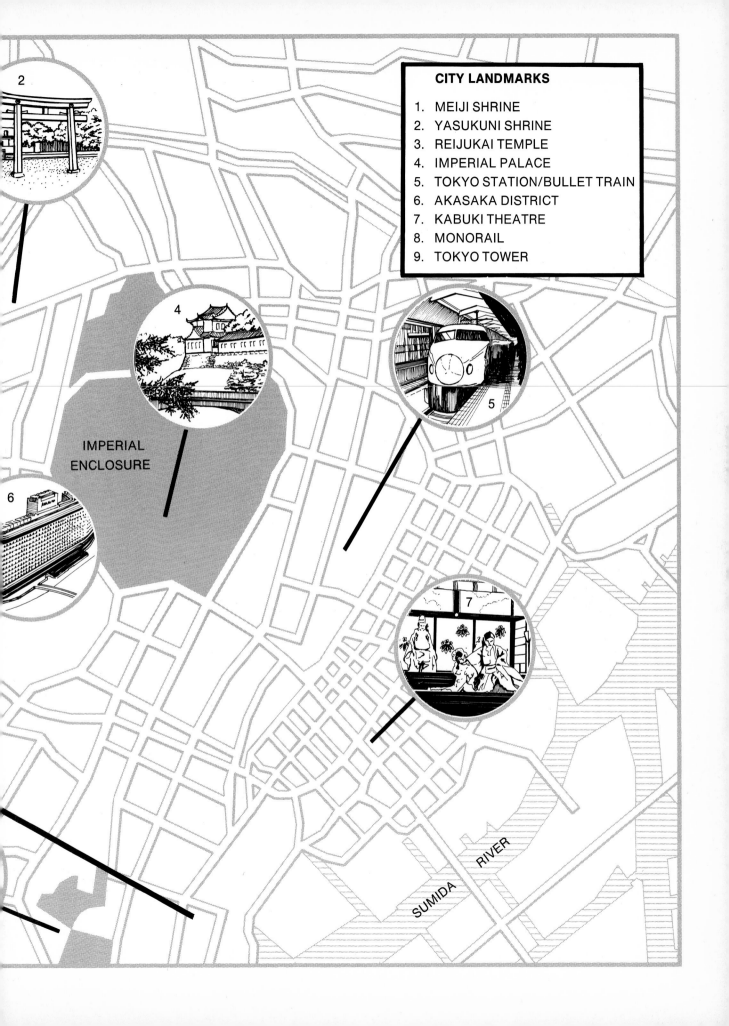

CITY LANDMARKS

1. MEIJI SHRINE
2. YASUKUNI SHRINE
3. REIJUKAI TEMPLE
4. IMPERIAL PALACE
5. TOKYO STATION/BULLET TRAIN
6. AKASAKA DISTRICT
7. KABUKI THEATRE
8. MONORAIL
9. TOKYO TOWER

IMPERIAL
ENCLOSURE

SUMIDA   RIVER

Past and Present

In 1457 a warrior and poet called Ota Dokan built a castle in the Toshima district of Japan. The castle stood on the site now occupied by the Imperial Palace and overlooked the marshy lowlands of the Sumida River. Ota took the name of his castle from the scattered fishing village which lay at its feet.

That name was Edo – later to become Tokyo – and it means estuary or literally, 'a place which juts out'.

By the end of the 15th century Edo still numbered no more than 100 houses. But in 1603 the castle was taken over by Tokugawa Ieyasu. This marked the beginning of the area's development. Ieyasu, founder of the Tokugawa Shogunate, turned the castle into a military garrison, considerably extending and altering the existing structure.

Two and a half centuries later the Shogunate was overthrown and the monarchy restored. In July, 1868, Edo's name was changed to Tokyo and it became the capital of Japan. The following year Emperor Meiji moved his court there from Kyoto.

This signalled the start of a flood of western ideas and culture into the country – Tokyo in particular. The Japanese called this process of civilization and enlightenment *Bunmei Kaika.* They were obsessed with catching up with Europe and America: anything western was emulated, admired and whenever possible, shamelessly copied.

The general leaning towards western influences made Tokyo the Japanese centre of modern culture. New literary movements sprang up in the universities; Shakespeare's plays were translated by Tsubouchi Shoyo; Russian literature was introduced as well as German, English and French. In 1887 the Tokyo University of Fine Art and the Tokyo University of Music were established in Ueno, becoming the centres of artistic and musical training.

Freedom of speech and of the Press was also highly regarded. Many newspapers (shimbun) were founded in the first decades of the Meiji Era, mainly for the purpose of supporting certain political parties. Among these were the noteworthy *Nichi-Nichi Shimbun* and the *Tokyo Asahi Shimbun,* founded in 1872 and 1888 respectively.

Around the turn of the 20th century, a commercial centre was built in the Marunouchi 'inside castle', which was in fact situated in the outer moat zone of the castle. Although Osaka was still Japan's largest commercial centre, Tokyo was about to take over.

The growth of Tokyo was drastically checked by the great earthquake of September, 1923. The subsequent fire killed more than 100,000 people and destroyed 360,000 houses. A short time later, however, Tokyo was reconstructed; its streets were widened and new steel-and-concrete blocks put up. The city's growth continued until the Second World War.

Sakura, or cherry blossom, is the Japanese national emblem and has long been regarded as the flower of flowers. There are more than a dozen species of which Yamazakura, Someiyoshino and Higanzakura are the most popular.

8

The war changed everything, demolishing the old and giving birth to the new: the system of government; the constitution and laws; social structure; people's lives, morals, thoughts and manners. Tokyo was reborn as the centre of democratic government and of capitalism. What followed became known in the west as the Japanese economic miracle.

Tokyo is divided into 23 administrative wards and has a population of 11,373,000 (approx. a tenth of that of the whole country) within its 796 square miles. The city lies at the mouth of the Sumida River, facing Tokyo Bay which opens out on the Pacific Ocean. The whole metropolitan area, bordering on the Chiba Prefecture to the east, on the Saitama Prefecture to the north, on the Yamanashi Prefecture to the south-west and on the Kanagawa Prefecture to the south, stretches westward across the still developing residential district into the steep Okutama and Chichibu Mountains.

All international flights to Tokyo operate to and from Haneda Airport or Tokyo International Airport, in Ota-ku, about eight miles south-west of the city centre. A new international airport was built several years ago in Narita, Chiba Prefecture, to help control the ever increasing air traffic. However, a continuing dispute over compensation for those who live in the neighbourhood has made it impossible to use. Consequently, Haneda is, for the time being, Tokyo's only airport.

There is no international seaport in Tokyo. Ocean lines to the capital region operate to and from Yokohama, Kanagawa Prefecture, while some domestic services like Oshima and/or the Hachijojima line are operated to and from Takeshiba Pier near Hamamatsu-cho.

Above: Ice cream is very popular among the younger generation and ice cream sellers are found all over the city.

Right: Although Japan's biggest opposition party, the Socialist Party and middle-of-the-road parties like Komeito (Clean Government Party) and the Democratic Socialist Party are making steady gains in seats, the ruling Liberal Democrats have been in power for the past 30 years.

Left: In this overcrowded city a great many people are still forced to live and work under the elevated railway. Happily, though, their numbers are steadily decreasing.
Above: Tokyo's radio mast, situated in the Shiba Park is about 1,000 feet high – over 100 feet taller than the Eiffel Tower in Paris. It has been in operation since 1958.
Right: Instant photos! If you are a busy tourist, you can take a picture here, or have one taken for you. This is one of Tokyo's more lively districts.

Japanese National Railways (J.N.R.), helped by several private railways on outlying lines, maintain an efficient rail network throughout Japan. Where necessary, services are supplemented by ferries and buses, many of them owned by J.N.R. Shinkansen or bullet trains run from Tokyo to Hakata, Fukuoka Prefecture, covering the 730 miles in six hours 56 minutes.

The over-ground rail network of J.N.R. and the private railways are efficient and economic, as well as being ideal for exploring the metropolitan area. In the heart of the city the Yamanote line, (light green trains) runs in a complete circle, connecting all the chief termini to one another. The Chuo line (pink trains) runs between Tokyo Station and Takao right across the Yamanote line and through the old residential area in the west, with its branch one line operating between Tachikawa and Okutama. The Keihin-Tohoku line (light blue trains) operates between Ofuna, Kanagawa Prefecture, and Omiya, Saitama Prefecture, running alongside the Yamanote line between Shinagawa and Tabata. The Sobu line (yellow trains) operates between Mitaka in the west and Chiba in the Chiba Prefecture, running parallel to the Chuo line between Mitaka and Ochanomizu. The Joban line (green trains) runs between Ueno and the developing residential area in the north. The majority of the trains, which are designed for commuter traffic, with seating capacity being much less than their standing room, are fast, clean and not overcrowded, except during peak rush hour times. The underground rail network run by the Tokyo Subway Corporation and the City of Tokyo also covers the whole metropolis and is very convenient.

Tokyo's main roads are either circular or radial concentric loop roads which are numbered consecutively from the nearest one to the centre. They are designed for access north or east from south or west, particularly in the suburbs, without coming into the centre of Tokyo. The roads radiating from the city run out to the densely populated satellite towns scattered outside the metropolitan area. Nowadays the central area has what they call the Metropolitan Motorway, which has served to ease the heavy traffic a little. But Tokyo's roads are still a nightmare for drivers and families living nearby.

To the east of the Sumida River stretches an area of thick alluvial soil. It has settled as deep as 13 feet in some places as the groundwater has been drawn off for industrial purposes. This lowland area is called Zero Metre zone because it is below sea level; the area used to suffer heavily from typhoons, flood tides and earthquakes.

Higher land in the west of the metropolitan area consists of volcanic layers on top of sand and gravel, leading to the fertile soil of Kanto plain. To the south of Tokyo lies hilly land, varying in height from 164 to 656 feet. Since the 1960s it has been developed as a residential area for an expected population of 500,000. Further to the south and west stretch the highlands of Okutama and Chichibu, part of the Chichibu-Tama National Park, consisting of old geological formations separated by the Tama River and its tributary valleys. The steeper slopes are wooded and the foothills are terraced with cultivated fields; the river supplies Tokyo's water.

Below: Geisha girls, dressed in their colourful and traditional costume. They are trained, from an early age, to entertain men in Japan's tea houses. The girls also perform at social functions where they sing, dance and play musical instruments.
Right: This geisha girl is carrying out ikebana, the Japanese art of flower arranging. It is learned by most women, usually as a qualification for marriage.

The climate of Tokyo is generally mild, although the summers are extremely hot and humid. The mean annual temperature is 14.7°C (58.5°F). As in the monsoon zone, Tokyo has two windy seasons: in summer masses of warm, humid air from the Pacific which causes the rainy season, tsuyu or baiu as the Japanese call it, in June; in winter a flow of cold, dry air from Siberia, which causes strong freezing winds (karakkaze). Tokyo is usually visited by a few typhoons every year between June and October. The average annual rainfall is 62 inches compared with that of London, 25.32 inches, and of New York, about 40 inches.

Left: Like all Japanese cities, Tokyo is liberally dotted with shrines. This one is dedicated to Jizo-son, a bodhisattva who is believed to save suffering human beings in the world of 'no Buddha'.

Below: Chochin, or paper lanterns, is a form of lighting used more for nostalgic and commercial reasons than for religious and practical ones. These particular lanterns are lit by electricity and hang outside a restaurant.

Tokyo is situated in the Fuji volcanic chain and has two or three earthquakes of medium scale each year. It used to be said that it was impossible to build skyscrapers in Tokyo due to possible major earthquakes. The great Kanto earthquake in 1923, which caused vast damage to the eastern area of Tokyo, proved however, that the five storey wooden pagoda of Ueno and the stone walls of the Edo Castle moat had remained standing because they were built in such a way that the shockwaves were dispersed in various directions. Traditional wooden buildings did not use nails but tenon-and-mortice joints which because the timbers had dried out and become loose absorbed the external energy. The stone walls of the moat, on the other hand, were coarsely laid for the same reason.

Tokyo's first skyscraper, the Kasumigaseki building, was designed to have the same flexible structure. So far it has survived several medium scale earthquakes and nowadays other skyscrapers are being built in the busiest areas, such as Shinjuku and Ikebukuro.

Theoretically, a great earthquake will occur around Tokyo any time within the next 20 years, unless the accumulated earthquake energy beneath Tokyo Bay is somehow dispersed. If it were to hit central Tokyo, the casualties would be exceptionally high and the city's function as the nerve centre of Japan paralyzed. In 1973 Komatsu Sakyo, the country's leading science fiction author, wrote a book entitled *Nihon Chinbotsu* (The Sinking of Japan), in which he showed how the earthquake following a great volcanic eruption would destroy Tokyo. In fact, Tokyo is sinking year by year, especially in the eastern areas, the Zero Metre zone, partly because of mass consumption of groundwater and partly because of dangerous movement of the crust.

Above: The koto is a traditional musical instrument with 13 long silk strings, played mostly by kimono-clad women.

Left: The interior of Asakusa Kannon Temple. The worship of Kannon, or the goddess of mercy, became popular with the rise of the Buddhist Hokekyo sect. The temple is thought to have been founded in the seventh century.

Right: Meiji-Jingu, the most important Shinto shrine in Tokyo, is dedicated to the Emperor Meiji (1852–1912) and his wife the Empress Dowager Shoken (1850–1914).

About three quarters of the dwellings in Tokyo are made of wood with fire-proof concrete and steel houses gradually becoming more common. The style of these houses is a mixture of east and west. They have two or three living rooms furnished with tatami (reed mats) and shoji (paper sliding doors) separated by fusuma (sliding screens), and a lounge in European style. Throughout the whole metropolitan area, there are many housing developments being undertaken by the Japanese Housing Corporation, the City of Tokyo and also by private building concerns.

19

Left: Children going into the Meiji-Jingu (jingu means shrine). The huge Inner Garden is thickly covered by old trees.
Below: A Shinto ceremony for a newly born baby at the Meiji-Jingu. Shinto is unusual in that it has no special doctrines or teachings.

All the large newspapers, publishers and broadcasting companies have their head offices in Tokyo. *Asahi Shimbun* which achieved the highest circulation in the world of 11,171,790 copies in March 1976; *Mainichi Shimbun* and *Yomiuri Shimbun* are the so-called Big Three of the Japanese newspapers. A daily economics journal called *Nihon Keizai Shimbun,* several papers in English and Korean and many popular sports and entertainments papers are all published in Tokyo. Dozens of other daily and weekly papers are also printed and distributed, as well as various kinds of weekly magazines. Tokyo has about ten television channels of both V.H.F. and U.H.F.; almost all programmes are televised in colour. N.H.K., the Japanese Broadcasting Corporation, is the only public broadcasting authority. There are also more than 60 radio stations.

The language of Tokyo is generally regarded as standard Japanese, although this is not strictly correct. In fact the Tokyo dialect is the basis of the common Japanese, or Kyotsu-go which is a form of speech designed for people throughout the whole of Japan. The famous accent of downtown Tokyo, the Beranmee, is appreciated as clear and lively by the people of Tokyo, and at the same time thought coarse and unrefined by the people of Osaka. It is possible to say, however, that the Tokyo dialect has served as a nucleus of the common Japanese, providing the country with political unity and a standardized education.

Left: A traditionally clad Japanese girl advertising a theatrical performance.
Above: Barges on the Sumida River. In old days the river was also called Ookawa (Big River) and carried heavy traffic. It was once so polluted that no fish could survive

in it for long. Now, however, it has been cleaned up considerably. *Right:* A father carrying his baby like this is a fairly rare sight in Tokyo.

Festival City

In the hustle and bustle of city life, a series of New Year's celebrations are a good opportunity to remind people of the old days. Like many other cities in Japan, the streets of Tokyo are gaily decorated and the girls wear colourful kimonos and display traditional hairstyles.

The most exciting event during the first seven days of the New Year is the Dezomeshiki, or parade of firemen. Tokyo has always been troubled with fire and the firemen have long been regarded as heroes. During the parade they dress in traditional costumes and perform acrobatic stunts on tall bamboo ladders.

At the beginning of summer, festivals or feasts, or matsuri as the Japanese call them, are held: traditional pageants with huge covered litters parading through busy streets. One of the largest and most exciting is Sanno Matsuri which originated in the Edo Era. Bon festival is a good occasion for family reunions. During the festival lanterns are lit for souls who, according to Buddhist belief, come back to this world

As amusement on summer nights, people have enjoyed firework displays since the Edo Era. The firework show at Keio Tamagawa on the Tama River during August has taken the place of the almost legendary one of Ryogoku on the Sumida River. It was abolished because it was thought too dangerous.

Among other historical festivals, the Tokyo Festival held in October is a newcomer which started only about 20 years ago. It celebrates the establishment of the autonomous municipality of Tokyo in 1898. A number of events such as the Tokyo Harbour Festival and the Miss Tokyo contest are featured.

During November, the Tori-no-ichi or Cock Fairs of Otori Shrine, Asakusa, are held on the cock days according to the Chinese animal calendar. People buy kumade, or bamboo rakes, for their happiness and business prosperity. The bigger the kumade they buy, the more prosperity they achieve. Therefore, people spare no expense.

With the approach of the New Year, Toshi-no-ichi or year-end markets are held at the Asakusa Kannon and Yagenbori Fudo Temples; various kinds of New Year decorations are arranged on every stall.

Tokyo's streets are hung with coloured banners to celebrate the festival of Tanabata on July 7th. This is the Star festival when, according to Japanese folklore, the cowherd Altair meets his lover, Vega the weaver, in the Milky Way.

24

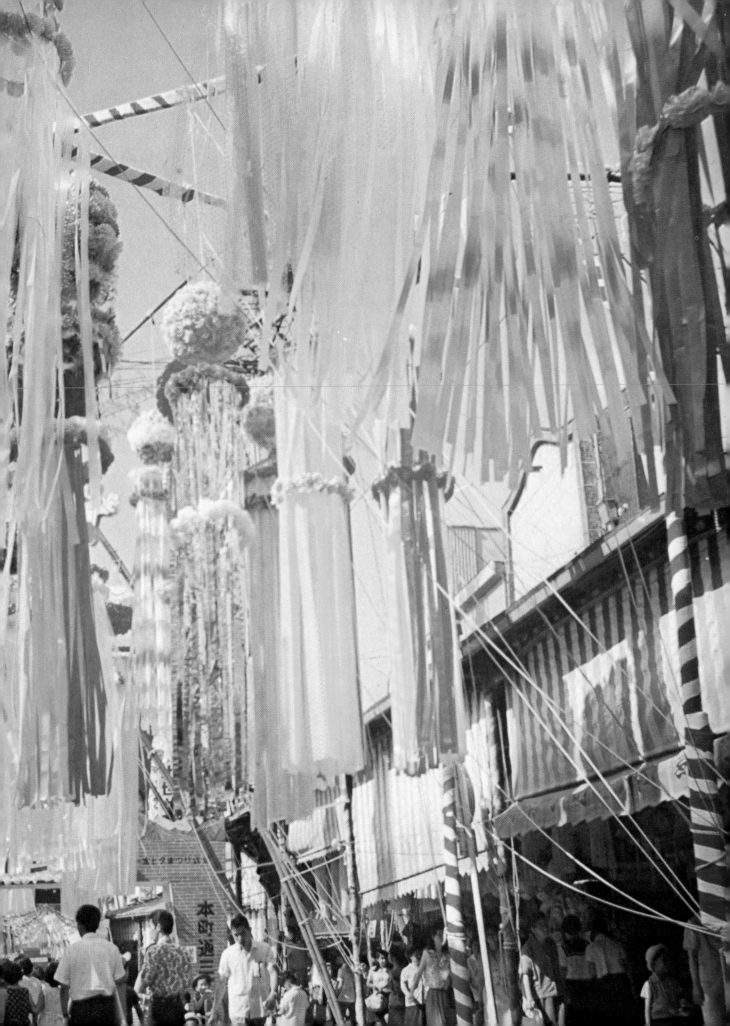

Above: Children's Day is celebrated on May 5th. Families with little boys festoon their houses with paper or cloth carp strung on bamboo poles.
Right: A street full of people in traditional dress taking part in the Nebuta Matsuri festival.

Below: Shrine palanquins, or covered litters, are paraded through the streets during the Ningyo Kuyo festival.
Right: Traditionally clad men celebrating a Shinto festival.

Cultural Tokyo

Tokyo has fewer cultural legacies than Kyoto and Nara. But it is impossible to ignore the inheritance from the Edo Era, when a unique culture flourished under the policy of seclusion. And, since the opening up of Japan, Tokyo has been the gateway to western culture. During the Meiji Enlightenment Period, for instance, Rokumei-kan, situated in central Tokyo, played the role of a social club where evening parties and balls were held for foreign diplomats and the aristocracy. Western manners and customs were rapidly introduced among commoners too. Since then Japanese culture has been greatly influenced by the west.

People in Tokyo have more opportunity to come into contact with western culture than elsewhere in Japan. Western music and dance are performed in various places. Many public institutions, such as the National Museum of Western Art, the Metropolitan Gallery of Fine Art, and department stores, hold various kinds of art exhibitions. The Bridgestone Gallery, owned by the Bridgestone Tyre Company, boasts a collection of 18th and 19th-century paintings of international renown. Another large private collection of unusual oriental *objets d'art* and antiques can be seen in the Nezu Art Museum. The largest museum in Japan, of course, is Tokyo's National Museum.

A taste for traditional culture, such as flower arranging and tea making, can also be satisfied. Lovers of traditional theatre are also catered for. The No, a highly stylized and abstract masque with dance and song, is regularly performed at Suidobashi Nogakudo and Yarai Nogakudo. Kabuki, a popular drama with dance and song, is performed by men only at Kabuki-za. Bunraku, a puppet drama with Joruri song, is performed at the National Theatre near the Imperial Palace.

There are numerous universities and colleges in Tokyo: among them the state-owned Tokyo University, the main buildings of which are situated in Bunko-ku. It is not only an academic symbol but also the epitome of the social structure of present-day Japan.

More than 50 per cent of high-school leavers go on to university or college and almost half of them gather in Tokyo. In addition to the 100 year old Tokyo University, there is Tokyo Kogyo University (engineering); Hitotsubashi University (trade and commerce); Tokyo University of Education and Tokyo Geijutsu University (music and art).

Besides these state-owned universities, there are many noteworthy private ones with their own unique method of study and/or education in some scientific field. These include Meiji, Chuo and Nihon in the so-called Latin Quarter near Kanda, Waseda and Keio.

Kabuki is a highly regarded art form which originated during the Edo Era in the latter half of the 16th century. This shows a scene from a performance in Tokyo. All the parts are played by men.

Above: Tokyo's Kabuki-za theatre, home of Kabuki. The theatre is situated in Ginza and was opened in 1889. It seats 2,216.
Right: Dance and music play an important role in Kabuki's highly stylized drama. The musicians mainly use a three-stringed balalaika-like instrument called a shamisen.

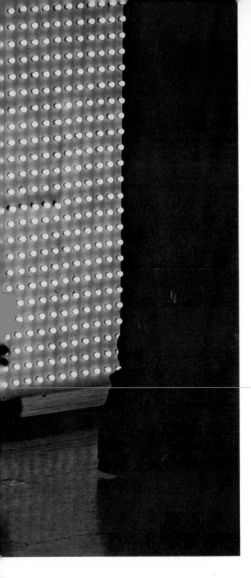

Left: A bird dance. The performers are imitating cranes – sybols of longevity.
Above: A revue at the Kokusai Theatre in Asakusa. In contrast with Kabuki drama, both men and women take part.
Right: The humble umbrella is being used as a prop in this ancient Japanese folk dance.

Below: A folk dance with a fan and a wand for exorcising evil spirits.
Right: The Tokyo National Museum is the largest museum in Japan and contains approximately 86,000 exhibits associated with the history and culture of Japan, China and India.

Right: The Meiji Memorial Picture Gallery in the Meiji Shrine Outer Garden. The approach road, designed so as not to damage the beauty of the garden, has been said to remind the British of The Mall in London.

The Economic Miracle

The Marunouchi-Tokyo station-Nihonbashi district, stretching to the east of the Imperial Palace, is the city's main business and financial area. Important trading companies known as sogo shosha, banks, insurance companies, stock brokers and similar establishments are all concentrated in this district, the nerve-centre of Tokyo, which epitomizes the Japanese economic miracle after the war.

Nihonbashi was the centre of trade even in the Edo Era: from here radiated the five high roads like Tokaido and Nakasendo. Echigoya, the present Mitsukoshi Department Store, was running a business as a clothing and dry goods store. The rivers and canals were crowded with boats coming from Osaka and other major coastal regions. Before and since the war the place has been a centre for department stores and wholesalers.

Around the turn of the century a commercial centre was built in the Marunouchi district, consisting of red-brick buildings of three or four storeys. After the war, with rapid economic growth, the area has become swollen; Maru-biru, an eight storey building, was the forerunner of Japanese economic growth. Many companies moved their head offices here from Osaka, which had previously been the largest trading town in Japan. Nowadays rows and rows of solid western-style buildings are competing in size and magnificence. At the same time the business district itself is expanding towards the neighbouring section, Kasumigaseki, the political centre of Japan.

During the daytime the district is crowded with white-collar workers who commute enormous distances, from as far away as Gunma and Yamanashi. The shortage of housing has driven people far from the city. Every morning thousands of people travel in packed trains. During the rush hours at every junction students, hired for the purpose, push passengers into the trains. In spite of these uncomfortable conditions, people want to work in the district. At night, in striking contrast to the day, it becomes a kind of no-man's-land peopled only with night-watchmen.

Japan is now the world's leading shipbuilding nation. In 1972 the *Globtik Tokyo,* then the world's largest oil tanker (483,000 tons), was launched from one of her 1,000 shipyards. This shows an aerial view of Tokyo's busy dockland.

Below: Marunouchi is Tokyo's nerve centre. Almost all the major banks and companies have their headquarters in this district.
Right: Kasumigaseki Building, the first earthquake-proof skyscraper in Japan, is modelled on an ancient five storey pagoda in Ueno Park, which withstood the great Kanto earthquake of 1923. So far, the Kasumigaseki Building has survived several earthquakes of medium scale.

Left: A pinball fanatic's paradise – one of Tokyo's amusement arcades.
Below: The Tokyo Securities Exchange in Kabuki-cho. It was reorganized in 1949 according to the Securities and Exchange Act of the same year.
Right: Every street in the city centre is busy with traffic all day long. The narrow road network causes congestion throughout Tokyo.

Left: Those citizens who cannot afford to, or who are unwilling to live near their place of work, are forced to travel from neighbouring districts, spending hours in the overcrowded trains.

Below: The main station at Shinjuku, a young and expanding outlying Tokyo district. As the terminus of two major private railways and the junction station of the National Railway, Shinjuku is rapidly becoming a thriving shopping and business centre.

Tokyo Sports

Judo, karate, aikido, kendo, sumo: these are the Japanese traditional sports. Sumo, Japanese wrestling, has been established as a national sport for centuries. Its origin springs from a legend that two gods wrestled in order to decide the ownership of a region. Sumo attained its position as a professional sport in the 1750s. Now, more than two centuries later, it is still one of the most exciting spectator sports.

The Kokugikan Hall, sumo's home base, has a seating capacity of 10,000 and is always full, especially on the final day of a 15-day tournament. Outside the hall colourful flags are lined up bearing the names of the wrestlers. Sumo has undergone only minor changes in rules and form throughout its long history and has maintained its great popularity, especially in downtown Tokyo, where people live in a more traditional and conventional manner.

Before each match both wrestlers stamp on the ring and bend their knees into a half-sitting posture. They then bow to each other and clap their hands. Afterwards they scatter a handful of salt over the ring – the old custom of purification – and toe the mark. This is repeated several times in a modified Shinto ritual. The fight is usually over in seconds.

It is more than a century since baseball was introduced from America. Now it has grown into the most popular participant and spectator sport for all ages. There are twelve professional teams in Japan, divided into two leagues, the Central and Pacific. Each team has its own stadium. The Mecca for baseball fans is the Korakuen Stadium, situated in central Tokyo. The stadium is owned by the Yomiuri Giants, probably the most popular team in Tokyo.

Apart from the professional teams, there are many baseball teams in the high schools, universities and the non-professional organizations.

Other traditional sports, karate or judo, for example, can be best seen in the Budokan Hall – an attractive building constructed in the traditional Japanese style at the time of the 1964 Tokyo Olympics.

A sumo wrestling match at the Kuramae Kokugikan stadium. Tournaments last up to 15 days and are televised live. The stadium seats 10,000 and is nearly always filled to capacity.

Left: Nippon Budokan Hall, modelled on the ancient Japanese style of architecture, stands in the vicinity of the Imperial Palace. It was used for the judo events in the Tokyo Olympic Games of 1964 and has been the centre of Japanese martial arts ever since.

Below: Japanese characters spelling karate – empty (kara), hand (te). Karate is a system of unarmed combat using the hands, feet, head and other parts of the body as weapons.

Below: A judo match between fathers and sons at the Kodo-kan Judo Hall. Here hundreds of Japanese and foreigners daily practise the art of self-defence known as judo (gentle way).

Left: Swimming, as is obvious here, is a popular Japanese pastime.
Below: Mr Kono, a black belt sixth dan, demonstrating the sometimes awesome art of karate by splitting a wooden block with his foot.
Right: Kendo, or ritual fencing, is another martial art which is practised by the majority of Japanese males. Here boy fencers are waiting to take part in a kendo competition.

Consumer Paradise

There are a great many department stores in Tokyo selling a wide variety of goods, from necessities to luxury articles. But there is another aspect. Throughout the year the stores hold exhibitions, sometimes of famous works of art from abroad. On Sundays or national holidays the crowds flock into the department stores to shop or just to see these exhibitions.

It is nearly ten years now since certain streets were designated pedestrian areas on Sundays. Ginza, the most fashionable avenue in Tokyo, teems with people strolling around the department stores and boutiques. It is the same in Shinjuku, although this is more popular with young people. The shopping streets run in all directions from the station; there is also the metro-promenade where all sorts of shops are found. If you don't want to go further than the station, you take a lift or escalator to the station building where anything you want can be bought. This is the same at all main stations.

The only thing missing is the sort of street markets which are so popular in London. But you can enjoy the lively downtown life in Nakamise Street at Asakusa. The long shopping arcade from the Kaminarimon Gate to the Sensoji Temple, is lined with souvenir shops. Here you will sense a different atmosphere from fashionable Ginza or the modern and youthful Shinjuku. Life is more traditional. Sometimes young people who are a little tired of the modern streets come here on a nostalgic visit.

Ameyoko Street is very lively. All sorts of goods are arranged casually in front of the shops. Just before the New Year, the street swarms with people looking for cheap provisions for the celebrations.

The recent big increase in living standards has given young people more to spend. Much of their money is spent on hi-fi equipment and the audio departments in the stores are always busy.

The bright lights of the consumer paradise. The narrow streets are festooned with numerous advertising signs and boards of every kind. No special restriction is imposed on the colour and method of street illumination in Tokyo.

Below: Asakusa Nakamise is one of the oldest and busiest shopping arcades in Tokyo. Many of the shops specialize in kimonos, their accessories, zori (sandals) and handbags.

Right: A window display in a kimono shop. Kimono, literally and in practice, means clothes of any kind. However it also describes the traditional costume of long, loose robes with wide sleeves.

Left: Artificial cherry blossom at
Kannon Temple, Asakusa.
Technology, it seems, is taking
over everywhere!
Below: Most Japanese are gadget-
crazy. The electrical shops are
always crowded with customers
buying anything from a
miniaturized television set, to the
latest, automatic washing machine.

Below: Ginza teems with extremely expensive general shops and stores selling a wide variety of high-quality goods. They include three major department stores, Mitsukoshi, Matsuzakaya and Matsuya.
Right: Akihabara is Tokyo's electrical appliance quarter.

Tokyo's Nightlife

Sakariba is a word which describes a district of bars, tea houses, restaurants, night-clubs, strip-clubs, discos, cinemas and theatres where nightlife is enjoyed in direct proportion to the money in your pocket.

In the Ginza area there are any number of bars noted for their expensive and exclusive atmosphere. Japanese-distilled Scotch costs more than £1 for a single measure: real imported Scotch is priceless! Street after street is crowded with department stores, tea houses, boutiques, haberdasheries, shoe shops, fruit shops and restaurants: every shop boasts of the fact that they are in Ginza. To satisfy their pride, therefore, you sometimes have to pay £2.50 for a single dish of avocado.

Politicians and company executives who are connected with the government frequent a place called Akasaka. It is more exclusive than Ginza; Akasaka contains many traditional restaurants or ryoutei as the Japanese call them. They are reserved for V.I.Ps. Money is important in Akasaka but not as important as position and influence.

Roppongi has two different faces: one is just like that of Akasaka, symbolized by exclusive and traditional restaurants, the other is more youthful and less exclusive. Restaurants and coffee shops, more European and/or seemingly more revolutionary, swarm with the so-called Roppongi-zoku (Roppongi-clique), some being intellectuals like writers, or university students.

Shibuya, Shinjuku and Ikebukuro, having rapidly developed after the war, have many common features: they are all termini of private railways with huge department stores owned by the same railway companies. There are a lot of 24-hour-open restaurants, tea houses, coffee shops and discos.

Asakusa is one of the oldest and most popular Sakariba in Tokyo. Once it was the main centre for all amusements: revues, light plays, comedies, films and even prostitution.

Ginza, Tokyo's most fashionable area, takes its name from gin (silver) and za (foundry), as 350 years ago, a silver foundry stood here.

Left: Endless night in Tokyo. Although many of the tea and coffee houses and restaurants close at eleven o'clock, the lights of Tokyo never quite go out.

Above: Night at Shinjuku, the city of the young which never sleeps. The 24-hour discos and coffee houses are crowded with students, hippies, artists and, as can be seen here, women plying the world's oldest trade.

Below: A crowded street in Asakusa. Asakusa Rokku is still loved by those people who remember the time when life was not quite so hurried.

Right: Pornographic productions saved the Japanese film industry from the slump it had fallen into as a result of the rise of television. There is a Japanese version of Linda Lovelace's *Deep Throat*, as well as one of *Emmanuelle!*

Below right: A cinema at Asakusa Rokku.

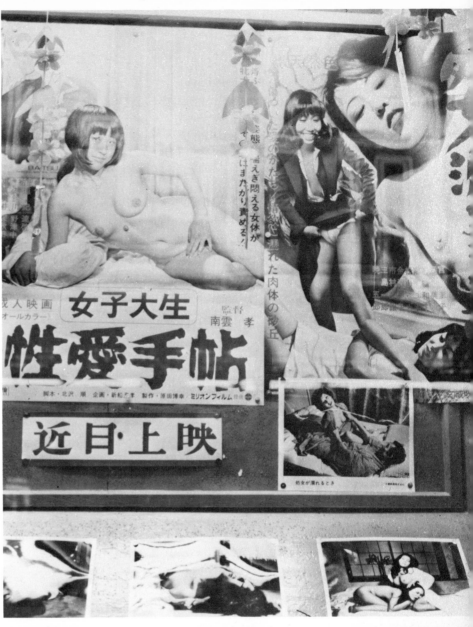

The Imperial Family

According to mythology the Japanese Empire was founded in 660 BC by Jimmu Tenno, a great-grandson of the Sun Goddess, Amaterasu, from whom all emperors were subsequently to claim descent. The myths were handed down and, until 1945, successive generations were taught that the present emperor, Hirohito, was the 124th emperor in direct descent from Jimmu Tenno.

The emperors were, in fact, worshipped as gods until Emperor Hirohito renounced his divinity in 1946. The emperor, in his capacity as the representative of the Sun Goddess on earth, was a reigning sovereign without power during the Shogunate. Successive emperors were to reign in Kyoto while the government of the country was carried out by the Shogunate in Edo, present-day Tokyo.

After the overthrow of the Tokugawa Shogunate and the emperor had been restored to power, Tokyo became the imperial centre of Japan. The emperor moved his court to the present Imperial Palace, formerly the castle of the Tokugawa Shogunate, from Kyoto in 1869. During the Meiji era, literally meaning enlightened government, the tenno system was established; in other words, the emperor was given almost absolute power, although it was the bureaucracy that actually ruled.

The present emperor is the third occupant of the throne since the Meiji Restoration. Under the terms of the new constitution, Hirohito is the symbol of the state and national unity. Apart from public duties, he spends his time studying biology and is noted for his researches into moss.

In spite of Hirohito's present, more ordinary existence, he was brought up in traditional seclusion, although his children have been given more freedom. When Crown Prince Akihito married a bride of his own choosing, in 1959, a commoner, of neither imperial extraction nor of aristocratic birth, people showed their approval: the wedding was broadcast throughout Japan and the streets swarmed with people who wanted to see the beautiful bride. Now the crown prince and his family, living in Akasaka Palace, lead a more or less ordinary family life. Despite this popularization of the monarchy, it is still said to be secluded compared with the British monarchy.

The Imperial Palace with the Nijubashi, or Double Bridge, in front. The palace, once the castle of the Tokugawa Shogunate, is surrounded by a series of moats and covers an area of 250 acres in the heart of Tokyo.

Below: Tourists visiting the Imperial Palace. The palace consists of two separate buildings – one reserved for official royal functions and the other as an Imperial residence.
Right: The Music Pavilion, an impressive modern, tiled building in the grounds of the Imperial Palace.

Top, above and right: The main
buildings of the Imperial Palace
were destroyed during the last war.
Reconstruction was completed
only as recently as 1968. The
palace has been in official use since
April 1969. These parts are those
specially designed for official
functions.

Parks and Gardens

There are altogether 250 parks in Tokyo, the largest of which is Ueno Park with an area of 210 acres. The statue of Saigo Takamori, hero of the Meiji Restoration, stands there wearing a kimono with his dog on a lead beside him. The park also includes museums, galleries, zoological gardens and a library.

A cultural, as well as an historic atmosphere is engendered by the Toshogu shrine, built in the 17th century in memory of Shogun Ieyasu, founder of the Tokugawa Shogunate. The five storey pagoda in front of the shrine, survived the great Kanto earthquake of 1923 and dates back to 1639. In the south-west of the park, there is the Shinobazu Pond which is famous for lotus flowers.

In the vicinity of the Ueno Park, there are two famous landscape gardens: the Korakuen Garden and the Rikugien Garden, built by feudal lords. They feature stone lanterns, ponds, arched bridges and beautifully displayed plants. Next to the Korakuen Garden, there is the Korakuen Sports Centre which consists of a baseball stadium, swimming pool and amusement park.

Most of Tokyo's parks were laid out as private gardens for feudal lords and have become open to the public throughout the decades. Typical is the Shinjuku Gyoen National Garden, transferred to the state in 1949 and now a recreation ground. The garden, situated to the south-east of Shinjuku, which is a large shopping and amusement centre, is now a popular outing spot. After the garden is closed, people may wander towards the Meiji Shrine Outer Garden or Inner Garden. The former consists of a gallery and various sports facilities, including the National Stadium, the main stadium for the 1964 Olympics. The latter is thick with old trees and the southern part of the grounds is famous for an iris garden. It contains more than 80 varieties.

In spring, the gardens and parks are full of people who come to see the cherry blossom. In autumn, chrysanthemums bloom in every park and garden. One of the best known parks for chrysanthemum shows is the Hibiya Park, near the business centre.

Happo-en ornamental garden is famed throughout the world for its planned and delicate design.

Above: A fountain in Hibiya Park, inaugurated in 1903 as the first park in the much-admired European style.
Right: A waterfall in Otani Gardens. Many of Tokyo's better, high-class restaurants have their own landscaped gardens.

Left: The Koishikawa Botanical Gardens in Bunkyo-ku.
Right: Ueno Zoological Gardens, with an excited group of school children taking a walk with a baby ostrich. Among the zoo's other attractions are two giant pandas – Ran-ran and Kan-kan.
Below: Tokyo's pigeon population has increased dramatically thanks to the amount of food they are fed by tourists.

Below: Shinjuku Gyoen National Gardens, five minutes walk from Shinjuku station. The gardens were transferred to the State from the Imperial household to be a public recreation ground.
Right: Carp are admired by the Japanese for their strength and persistence. They are also considered very good to eat!

Old Tokyo

When Tokyo was known as Edo, it was a city of craftsmen and skilled workers whose livings were guaranteed by the state. Around the Edo Castle were distributed craftsmen's districts, each of which formed an exclusive society similar to the European guilds. The name of Ginza, for instance, means literally the foundry of silver and originates from the silver mint established there in 1612.

The engineers, carpenters, plasterers, tilers and other craftsmen who took a hand in repairing and remodelling Edo Castle (built in 1457 for Ota Dokan) in 1603, were not men of science and technology in a modern sense, but by heritage and their own experience were familiar with the best building methods. Today you can still see the beautiful parabolic curve of the outer layers of moat-stones as well as that of the roof of the castle. This curve serves to disperse external pressure or energy and protects the buildings from earthquakes.

To the south-east of the Imperial Palace there stands the Imperial Hotel. In contrast to the traditional beauty of the Edo Castle, that of the huge brick hotel is more European, reflecting the cultural trend of the Enlightenment Period of the early Meiji Era.

To the north of the Imperial Palace stretch old streets full of second-hand bookshops from Kudan-Shita to Surugadai-shita: people in Tokyo call this quarter Jinbo-cho. You would be lucky to find any really ancient books. Even a ten year old book is regarded as antique in Tokyo. However, the musty atmosphere which pervades each shop is a constant reminder of the nostalgia of the days of the Meiji Enlightenment and Taisho Democracy.

Nowadays there is virtually nothing old left in Tokyo: it is, of course, possible to come across some architecture, streets and parks which seem to proclaim their age, but they mean virtually nothing – just skeletal oldness, mere nostalgia. It is true that the Japanese in general tend to reject and exclude anything old or traditional as old-fashioned, but Tokyo's drastic reformation and modernization is due to two ruinous factors; the great Kanto earthquake of 1923 and the perpetual air-raids during the Second World War, which destroyed more than 700,000 buildings.

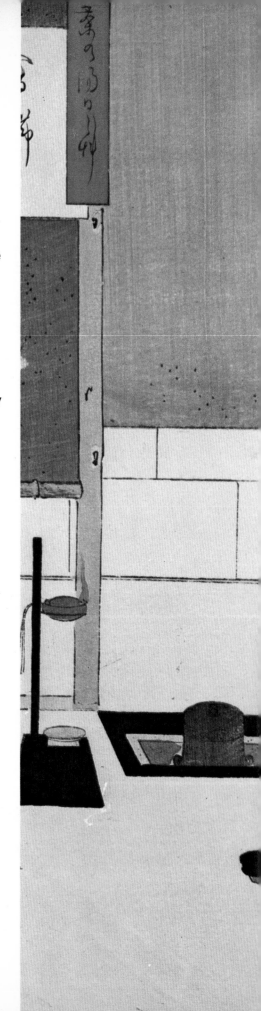

An old print of a Japanese tea ceremony. The art of cahnoyu (tea making) was perfected by Sen-no-Rikyu (1522–1591). Nowadays many young girls acquire the skill as a qualification for marriage.

Below: Times past in Ginza. The trams and rickshaws have long since vanished and are now more usually to be found in novels and stories of old days.
Right: A performance of ancient music and dance dating back to the seventh century.

Overleaf: The Three Horsemen, a print by Katsushika Hokusai (1760–1849). Hokusai was a famous Ukiyoe, or woodcut exponent, together with Hiroshige and Utamaro. His genius can be seen mostly in landscape prints.

冨嶽三十六景
隅田川
関屋七里

畫北斎の筆

Left: An old engraving of a cash-
and-carry shop dating back more
than 100 years.
Above: An old photograph showing
an Asakusa street market as it once
was.

Away From it All

Musashino is an area which extends from Kawagoe City in the Saitama Prefecture down to the Tama River and then eastward to the Ara River. It was once thickly covered with woodlands but has been developed with such speed that only a few patches in the west have been left for recreational purposes.

Old Musashino, or traces of it, can be found in the Chichibu-Tama National Park. Several reservoirs, like Okutama-ko, Tama-ko, and Sayama-ko are not only sources of water supply for Tokyo, but suitable places for a one-day excursion from the city.

Mount Takao is a popular hiking spot, convenient transport being available. On the mountain top there is a small temple among old trees. Fresh green in spring and scarlet-tinged in the autumn, the area attracts many hikers.

Tamagawa Recreation Park, Toshima-en and Yomiuri-land are just a few examples of the numerous parks outside the city. Seibu-en is also a well organized park, noted for the Unesco village, where you can find replica houses from all over the world. Another suitable place for a family outing is the Tama Zoological Garden and safari park, where lions and other animals are kept in the open.

In the western region of Tokyo, traces of Musashino are found: Inogashira Park, Shakujii Park and Jindaiji Botanical Gardens.
The Izu-shichito or Izu-Seven-Islands, situated in the Pacific Ocean to the south-west of Tokyo Bay, are beautiful resorts, washed by the warm Black Current. Oshima, the largest island, is noted for Japanese camellias blooming in the early spring; red flowers, seen among dark green thick leaves, attract tourist's eyes. Another spectacle of this island is Mount Mihara, the active volcano.

Further south, but still within an hour's flight from Tokyo, is Hachijo-jima. This was an island of the banished in the Edo Era, known as Hachijo-jima where even the birds dared not fly. Many sad songs of the banished, yearning for their loved ones have been passed down from generation to generation. Today Hachijo-jima is a happy place with blue seas and clear skies.

A beautiful tiered pagoda with the snow-capped peak of Mount Fujiama rising in the background.

Left: The camellia tunnel of Oshima. The biggest of the Izu-Seven-Islands, Oshima is noted for its active volcano Mihara-yama and tsubaki, or Japanese camellias, which are not only beautiful to look at, but produce a cosmetic oil.
Below: Meoto-iwa, or 'wedded rocks', in Ise-Shima National Park. The new Tokaido bullet train makes the journey from Tokyo in less than three hours.

Above: Mount Shirane in the Nikko National Park. Nikko is particularly noted for a magnificent 17th-century shrine which is dedicated to Tokugawa Ieyasu, the founder of the Tokugawa Shogunate and for its natural beauty. It is less than two hours from Asakusa by train.
Right: Mount Zao in Tohoku, is a well-known winter sports resort.

Changing Tokyo

Change in Tokyo is sudden and rapid. The people are quite accustomed to relinquishing the out-of-date and the impractical for the sake of modernization and economic growth.

Until just 20 years ago all the main streets in Tokyo were covered with a network of trams which have now been replaced by buses and the underground railway. Although the trams were slow and noisy, they never polluted the city. Now motor cars, the symbol of the Japanese economic miracle, kill trees with their exhaust fumes.

Large parts of Tokyo were destroyed by air raids during the Second World War but afterwards the city grew rapidly. Shinjuku, Shibuya and Ikebukuro are now large shopping and amusement centres, when once they were the dreary outskirts of Tokyo. The formerly bleak Shinjuku area has prospered and become the city's second largest commercial district, with skyscrapers like the 46 storey Keio Plaza Hotel which stands on the demolished site of a filtration plant. There is a splendid view of the city from the observation platforms of the 1,000 feet high Tokyo Tower, a multi-purpose radio tower on a rise of the Shiba Park.

With the rapid development of the city, its population has increased year by year. The shortage of housing has driven people out of the city and at the same time the improvement of various commuting facilities has dispersed them even further. Tokyo's eastern and north-eastern suburbs have, therefore, been growing into residential areas. The suburbs show the results of a rather short-sighted housing policy: seemingly crushed houses ranging from tiny shacks to huge blocks of flats. Woods and forests are being destroyed and replaced by housing lots. Nowadays wild animals are only to be found, in the mountains.

Everything in Tokyo changes rapidly; window displays of the department stores are altered every week. Even a piece of ten year old furniture can be regarded as a rare antique. Amidst rubbish piled up by the roadside you will find refrigerators and television sets that are still in good condition.

Everyone seems to believe that waste is a virtue. The economic miracle has changed not only the city itself but the people's morality. Whoever visits Tokyo after a short absence will find himself to be a *Urashima Taro* who, according to Japanese folklore, became an old man when he returned to his home town after spending a cheerful three years in the sea god's palace.

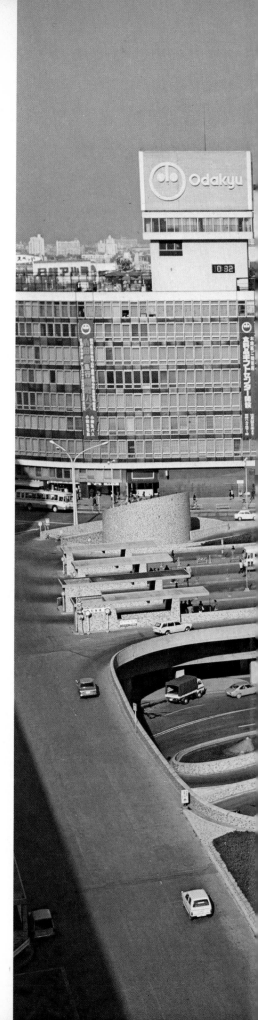

The west gate of Shinjuku station. Shinjuku's west side is expanding rapidly and is often referred to as fuku-toshin, the second city-centre.

Left: The monorail running between Hamamatsu-cho and Haneda Airport is the fastest way to reach the airport. The motorways are almost always blocked with lines of traffic.
Below: The monorail speeding to its terminus at Hamamatsu-cho.

Left: The Akasaka Hotel is one of Tokyo's many top-class hotels.
Below: This bullet train covers the 730 miles between Tokyo and Hakata in 6 hours and 56 minutes. The service between Osaka and Okayama, inaugurated in 1972, claims to be the world's fastest point-to-point schedule. The 110 mile journey takes just one hour.